Postcards from Checkpoint Charlie

Postcards from

Checkpoint Charlie

Introduction by
Andrew Roberts

Bodleian Library
UNIVERSITY OF OXFORD

The Bodleian Library would like to thank the following for their assistance in producing this book: John Fraser, John Pinfold, Kathrin Lutz, Dirk Lenhart, Ernst Volland, Wolfgang Skowronski, Jürgen Koch, and Alfred Folkers.

First published in 2008 by the Bodleian Library
Broad Street
Oxford OX1 3BG

www.bodleianbookshop.co.uk

ISBN 13: 978 1 85124 322 8

The John Fraser Collection of Propaganda Postcards is part of the John Johnson Collection of Printed Ephemera in the Bodleian Library.

Designed by Dot Little
Printed in Slovenia by Impress dd
British Library Catalogue in Publishing Data
A CIP record of this publication is available from the British Library

Collector's Foreword

From an early age I was interested in history. My mother gave me my first postcard, of King George VI at his coronation. When she took me to St Paul's Cathedral, I bought a postcard of Nelson's statue. In 1944 my local Woolworths sold sepia photographic postcards of generals Eisenhower, Alexander, and Montgomery. From then on I was a compulsive collector of any postcards of a historical or current political interest.

I was strongly influenced by the example of my artist aunt, Helen McKie (pronounced to rhyme with key). She had a large collection of postcards, mainly of views, arranged in order of country and subject matter, which she used for reference purposes. So I had her example to follow, and after her death I acquired her postcards of Hitler (she was the first woman artist to be allowed in the Brown House when she was commissioned to do a series on Germany in 1932 for the *Sketch*) and also cards of Rome with its Fascist décor. (There is an entry for her in *Who Was Who* for the 1950s.)

John Fraser, London

Introduction

On Sunday 13 August 1961, the inhabitants of Berlin woke up to a very disconcerting sound. In the early hours, East German troops had taken up station all along the twenty-six-mile border between the Russian sector of the city in the east and the British, American, and French sectors in the west – as demarcated at the end of the Second World War – and construction workers were beginning to build a wall along it. The population left their homes to watch what was happening; they were witnessing nothing less than the erection of the physical manifestation of the Cold War division between Capitalism and Communism.

In the sixteen years since 1945, the pluralistic, democratic values of free-market West Germany had produced an economic miracle that had brought high and rising standards of living to those fortunate to live on that side of the Iron Curtain. In East Germany, however, the authoritarian, sclerotic command-economy imposed by the USSR had delivered little in the way of material benefits. The migration of many of East Germany's brightest young people, eager to make new lives in the West, persuaded the Russians and their East German satellite that this could not go on.

Instead of making the Eastern European countries more attractive to live in through political, social, and economic liberalization, the Communist rulers of the Warsaw Pact – who all took their orders from Moscow – instead imprisoned their populations behind the Iron Curtain. The most tangible and brutal manifestation of this was the Berlin Wall, as it was known in the West, or the 'Anti-Fascist Protective Rampart' as it was dubbed by the GDR leaders. Once extended the full ninety-six miles around the whole of the Western sectors of Berlin – and with the penalty for unauthorised crossing being death – the contrast between the Free World and Communist tyranny could not have been more stark.

Families were split on either side of the Wall; emigration from the East was cut to a trickle; searchlights, watchtowers, machine-gun posts, and barbed wire were used to prevent East Germans escaping across the Wall to freedom. Although around five thousand people succeeded in crossing it in the twenty-eight years of its existence – the vast majority in the first few months – it is believed that over 160 people were killed in the attempt.

One of the most moving of the highly evocative postcards in this superb collection depicts the mountains of flowers laid in memory for one such would-be escapee. The most famous was the uniformed East German officer Conrad Schumann, whose leap across the barbed wire on 15 August 1961, complete with his rifle slung over his back, was captured on film, and is in this collection. It became an iconic image. The last person to die trying to cross was Chris Gueffroy, who was killed as late as 6 February 1989, only ten months before the Wall fell.

There were eight official crossing places – or checkpoints – between East and West Berlin once the Wall was erected, where documentation would be checked by the East German guards before anyone was allowed in or out of East Berlin. By far the most famous of these was Checkpoint 'Charlie' on the Friedrichstrasse between the American and Soviet sectors, which was immortalized in hundreds of books, films, documentaries, and spy-dramas. These postcards show how little the checkpoint itself changed over the nearly three decades of its notoriety, a wooden shed that in the 1980s was finally replaced by a slightly more permanent metal structure, ironically just as permanence was no longer necessary. (The nickname 'Charlie' was not named after anyone, but was merely NATO's phonetic word for the letter 'C'.)

Checkpoint Charlie was the generally acknowledged front line between Communism and the Free World, and in 1973 it was fired upon by East German border guards, creating an instant international incident. Today it can be seen in a Berlin museum. Famed in part because of the number of times it appears in spy books of the John Le Carré mould – where spies were exchanged between the KGB and Western intelligence agencies – in real life Checkpoint Charlie was only used by Westerners going into the East, and not in the other direction.

Soon after the Wall was built, President John F. Kennedy visited to show his solidarity with West Berlin, famously proclaiming himself to be an honorary citizen with the words: 'Ich bin ein Berliner.' It was a reminder to the Soviets that even situated as it was deep within East German territory, West Berlin was as much a part of the West in 1961 as it had been when the Truman administration had gone to its aid during the Berlin Airlift in 1948. Ronald Reagan went one stage further than J.F.K., when in June 1987 he urged Mikhail Gorbachev: 'Mr General Secretary, tear down this wall!' A photograph in this collection shows Reagan looking through the metal bars of one part of the Wall. By that time, much of the Western side of the Wall was covered in graffiti art celebrating liberty, also displayed in this publication.

Several of these postcards – nearly all of which were collected over decades by one of the greatest of all British postcard collectors, John Fraser, and generously donated to the Bodleian Library at Oxford – are evocative of that seminal moment on 9 November 1989 when the Wall was indeed finally torn down, the most powerful of all the many signals that year that the Communist Party of the Soviet Union would no longer use force to defend its power and privileges. The reuniting of East and West Berlin that night and over the following weeks and months, often with scenes of great exuberance as young people danced on the Wall and celebrated its demise, presaged the reunification of Germany itself, which took place the following October. By then what the Germans called 'Mauer-Spechte' (wall peckers) had demolished much of the structure, for sale as souvenirs, paperweights and paraphernalia all over the world.

Those who escaped East Berlin through tunnels, in microlite planes, by hot-air balloon, and other means, showed the willingness of the human spirit to take risks – even mortal ones – in order to be able to live in freedom. The Bodleian's fine reproduction of these fascinating and moving postcards is a tribute to their courage, and a memorial to those like Chris Gueffroy who died in attempt.

Andrew Roberts

The Postcards

BERLIN

Sowjetische Soldaten hissen die Siegesfahne auf dem Reichstagsgebäude, 2. Mai 1945 · Soviet soldiers hoist the victory flag on the Reichstag, 2 May 1945 · Soldados soviéticos enarbolan la bandera de la victoria sobre el edificio del Reichstag, 2 de mayo de 1945

Photo: bpk Berlin · © publicon Verlagsgesellschaft mbH · Am Festungsgraben 1 · 10117 Berlin

publicon
B 119

Soviet soldiers hoist the victory flag on the Reichstag, 2 May 1945

Seemingly spontaneous, but in fact carefully choreographed, this photograph has become an iconic image of the Soviet victory over Nazi Germany in the Second World War. A week earlier American and Russian forces had met on the Elbe, thus setting the scene for the post-war division of Germany into zones occupied by the victorious allies.

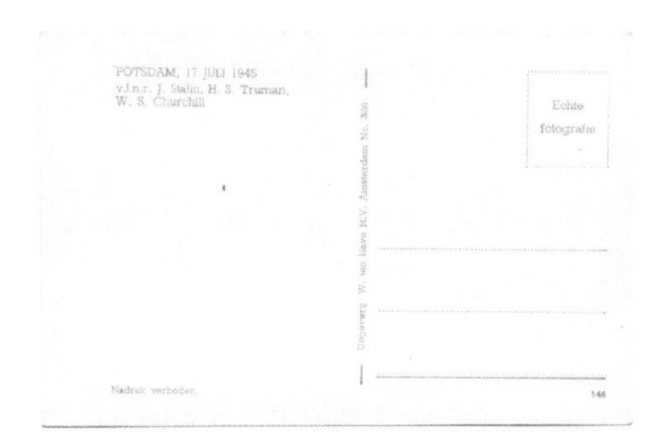

Stalin, Truman, and Churchill at the Potsdam Conference, 1945

At the end of the Second World War the three victorious Allied leaders, Stalin, Truman, and Churchill, met at the former royal palace of Schloss Cecilienhof in Potsdam to determine the future of Germany. The Potsdam Conference lasted from 17 July to 2 August 1945, with Churchill being replaced by Clement Attlee after the result of the British General Election was announced on 26 July.

As well as moving Germany's eastern border westwards to the Oder–Neisse line, the Allied leaders confirmed the decision, made at Yalta, to divide both Germany and Austria into four zones of occupation (the French were allotted the fourth zone), and to divide the capital cities of Berlin, and Vienna in a similar way. This was intended initially as only a temporary measure until a final peace treaty could be signed, but in the event the fundamental differences in outlook between the Western Allies and the Soviet Union meant that no formal treaty ending the Second World War in Europe was signed until the end of the Cold War forty-five years later. Although the four-power occupation of Vienna was ended in 1955, the occupation of Berlin was to last throughout the whole of that period.

This card is unusual in showing Stalin smoking a cigarette; in his public image, he usually preferred to be depicted as a pipe smoker.

Berlin Blockade, 1948/49. A 'Raisin bomber' coming in to land

The Berlin Airlift during 1948–49 represented the first major conflict between the Russians and the Western Allies during the Cold War. On 12 June 1948 the Soviets announced that the main autobahn linking Western Germany with West Berlin would be 'closed for repairs' and the rail links were also closed, because of 'technical difficulties', twelve days later. The aim of the Soviets was to blockade West Berlin and force the Western Allies to abandon it, but the British and the Americans determined to keep the city supplied by air. Between June 1948 and May 1949, when the blockade was lifted a total of 278,228 sorties were flown, carrying over two million tons of food and other goods into West Berlin. The success of the airlift was a major propaganda victory for the West, demonstrating both its industrial might and its commitment to West Berlin. As the American commander, General Clay put it: 'We are convinced that our remaining in Berlin is essential to our prestige in Germany and in Europe. For good or bad it has become a symbol of American intent.'

'Raisin bombers' were so called because some of the American pilots used to drop sweets and chocolates to groups of children as they came in to land, as shown here.

Berlin – Hauptstadt der DDR
Leninderkmal am Leninplatz
Берлин — столица ГДР
памятник Ленину у
площади Ленина
Berlin – Capital of the GDR
Lenin memorial on the Leninplatz
Berlin – Capitale de la R.D.A.
Monument de Lénine sur la Leninplatz

Foto: Berlin-Information
EVP: 0,25 M

VEB BILD UND HEIMAT REICHENBACH i. V.

Echt Foto

V 11 50 A 1/8 474/73 01 15 00 111 K

Lenin memorial on the Leninplatz

This view of a group of children dwarfed by the huge, sixty-foot high statue of Lenin, and the tower blocks behind, seems to encapsulate the nature of the East German state under Communism. The statue was made of Ukrainian granite and was unveiled in April, 1970. After the fall of Communism it was broken up into 129 pieces and buried under a mound of sand in a forest outside the city. Leninplatz was renamed Platz der Vereinten Nationen (Square of National Union) in 1992.

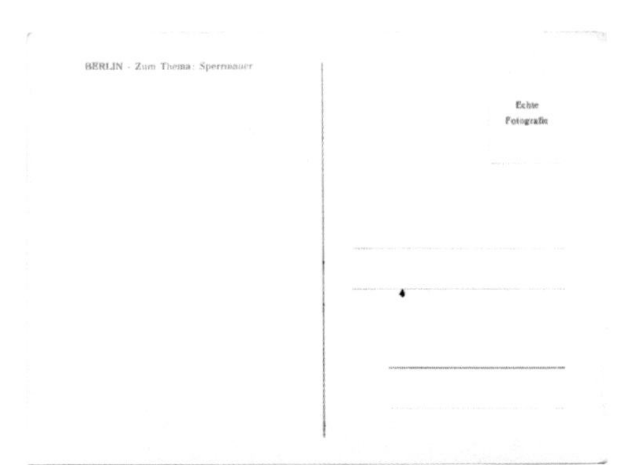

‘No one has the intention to create a wall’

Faced with an ever-increasing number of its citizens leaving to start a new life in the more affluent West, the East German government began to look at ways of preventing this exodus. On 15 June 1961, at an international press conference, the East German leader, Walter Ulbricht, announced that ‘No one has the intention to create a wall’, but just two months later, this was indeed the solution to the problem adopted by the East German authorities. Ulbricht’s statement was the first time the word ‘wall’ had been used to describe the division of the city.

Proletarier aller Länder vereinigt euch!

NEUES DEUTSCHLAND

ORGAN DES ZENTRALKOMITEES DER SOZIALISTISCHEN EINHEITSPARTEI DEUTSCHLANDS

„Ich verstehe Ihre Frage so, daß es in Westdeutschland Menschen gibt, die wünschen, daß wir die Bauarbeiter der Hauptstadt der DDR dazu mobilisieren, eine Mauer aufzurichten. Mir ist nicht bekannt, daß eine solche Absicht besteht. Die Bauarbeiter unserer Hauptstadt beschäftigen sich hauptsächlich mit Wohnungsbau, und ihre Arbeitskraft wird dafür voll eingesetzt.

Niemand hat die Absicht, eine Mauer zu errichten!“

Ulbricht am 15. Juni 1961

auf einer internationalen Pressekonferenz in Ostberlin

Herausgeber: Arbeitsgemeinschaft 13. August e.V.
im Ausstellungs-HAUS AM CHECKPOINT CHARLIE:
„DIE MAUER - vom 13. August zur heutigen Grenze"
„Geteilte Interpretationen - Maler sehen Die MAUER"
„BERLIN - von der Frontstadt zur Brücke Europas"
1000 Berlin 61, Friedrichstraße 44, Tel. 251 45 69, 251 69 02
Foto: Copyright, auch für nicht kommerzielle Zwecke

Sonntag, 13. August 1961, morgens
Waldemar- Ecke Luckauer Straße
in Berlin-Kreuzberg.

Sunday morning, 13 August 1961, Waldemarstrasse at the corner of Luckauer Strasse in Berlin-Kreuzberg

On the morning of 13 August 1961, a physical division between the two halves of Berlin was created for the first time. Initially the barrier consisted of no more than a barbed-wire fence, with armed guards manning the crossing points. Judging by the expressions on the faces of this group, they were resolute but also nervous and uncertain how to behave in this new situation.

Herausgeber: Arbeitsgemeinschaft 13. August e. V.
im MUSEUM HAUS AM CHECKPOINT CHARLIE:
- "DIE MAUER - vom 13. August bis heute"
- "Maler interpretieren DIE MAUER"
- "BERLIN - von der Frontstadt zur Brücke Europas"
- "VON GANDHI BIS WALESA - Gewaltfreier Kampf für Menschenrechte"

1000 Berlin 61, Friedrichstr. 44, Tel.: (030) 251 10 31
Fotos: Copyright, auch für nicht kommerzielle Zwecke

13. August 1961, 8 Uhr.
Eine Straßenseite in der Stadtmitte Berlins wird zur Grenze.

Nr. 9

13 August 1961, 8 o'clock. Waving in a street by the boundary in the Mitte district of Berlin

The slightly nervous wave of these children greeting their friends or neighbours on the other side of the fence in the first moments of the 'Wall' suggests the initial bewilderment of Berliners faced with this physical barrier across their city.

13. August 1961 in Berlin

Dieses Kind will hinüber. Der Posten hat Befehl, niemand durchzulassen. Trotzdem öffnet er den Draht. In diesem Augenblick sieht es der Vorgesetzte (Bild). Wegen seines Vergehens wurde der Posten sogleich abkommandiert.

This child wants to cross. The guard has orders to let nobody pass. Nevertheless he opens the barbed wire. At this moment (photo) his superior sees what is happening. Because of his acting contrary to the command he was immediately detached.

Herausgeber: Verlag Haus am Checkpoint Charlie Nr. 21

13 August 1961 in Berlin

The caption to this card reads: 'This child wants to cross. The guard has orders to let nobody pass. Nevertheless he opens the barbed wire. At this moment (photo) his superior sees what is happening. Because of his acting contrary to the command he was immediately detached.'

Herausgeber: Arbeitsgemeinschaft 13. August e.V.
im Ausstellungs-HAUS AM CHECKPOINT CHARLIE:
„DIE MAUER - vom 13. August zur heutigen Grenze"
„Geteilte Interpretationen - Maler sehen Die MAUER"
„BERLIN - von der Frontstadt zur Brücke Europas"
1000 Berlin 61, Friedrichstraße 44, Telefon 251 10 31
Foto: Copyright, auch für nicht kommerzielle Zwecke

14. 8. 1961 Bernauer Straße.
Der erste geflüchtete Volksarmist, einer
von 2800 seit dem Bau der MAUER. Nr. 1

14.8.1961. Bernauer Strasse. The first escape by a border guard

Just two days after the sector borders were closed, Conrad Schumann became the first serving East German border guard to defect to the West. The photograph was widely reproduced at the time and became an iconic image of the Cold War. Schumann was aged only 19 when he made his escape (on 15 August, not the 14th as the caption says) by jumping over the wire at the corner of Ruppinerstrasse and Bernauerstrasse. He later moved to Bavaria and said after the Berlin Wall fell, twenty-eight years later, that 'Only since 9 November 1989 have I felt truly free.' Suffering from depression, he committed suicide by hanging himself in 1998.

SECTEUR

"Checkpoint" at the foreigners' crossing point, Friedrichstrasse

After the Wall was put up eight border crossings were established between East and West Berlin. This is an early view of the famous Checkpoint Charlie, where the American and Soviet zones met in the heart of the city. Use of the different checkpoints was restricted to different nationalities, and Checkpoint Charlie could only be used by Allied personnel and non-German citizens.

US ARMY CHECKPOINT
YOU ARE LEAVING
THE AMERICAN SECTOR
VOUS SORTEZ
DU SECTEUR AMERICAIN
Berlin, Friedrichstraße
Ausländerübergang Friedrichstr., „Checkpoint"

Berlin, Friedrichstrasse, Soviet vehicle at Checkpoint Charlie, 1962

Another early view of Checkpoint Charlie. Charlie was so named because it was the third of the US army's checkpoints on the corridor between West Germany and East Berlin. Checkpoint Alpha was at Helmstedt where the autobahn crossed from West to East Germany, and Checkpoint Bravo was where it crossed from East Germany into West Berlin.

ALLIED CHECKPOINT
US ARMY CHECKPOINT

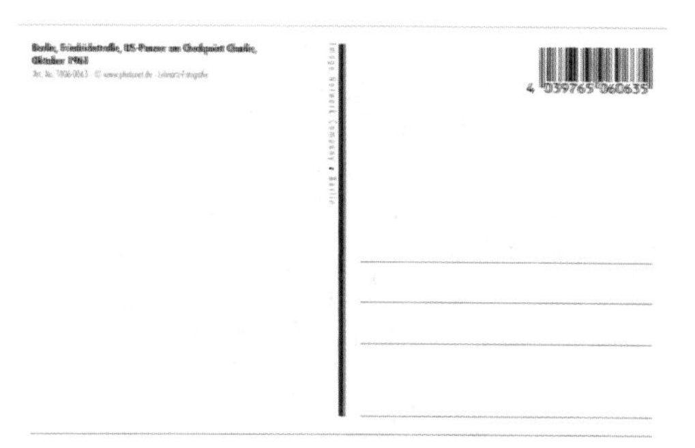

Berlin, Friedrichstrasse, US tanks at Checkpoint Charlie, October 1961

A series of diplomatic incidents that heightened the tension between the two superpowers resulted in a tense stand-off between American and Russian tanks at Checkpoint Charlie between 26 and 28 October 1961. As many as ten tanks on each side, loaded with live ammunition, faced each other across the border, and there was a real possibility of armed conflict. The situation was only diffused after Kennedy and Khrushchev had negotiated a face-saving formula, whereby the tanks gradually withdrew a few metres at a time.

As in 1948–49, the West had demonstrated its resolve to remain in West Berlin and the right of Allied personnel to travel unmolested into all sectors of the city, but there was also a tacit acceptance of the Wall as a fact of life. As Kennedy commented, 'It's not a very nice solution, but a wall is a hell of a lot better than a war.'

berg
stuben
FOTO-ZENTRUM

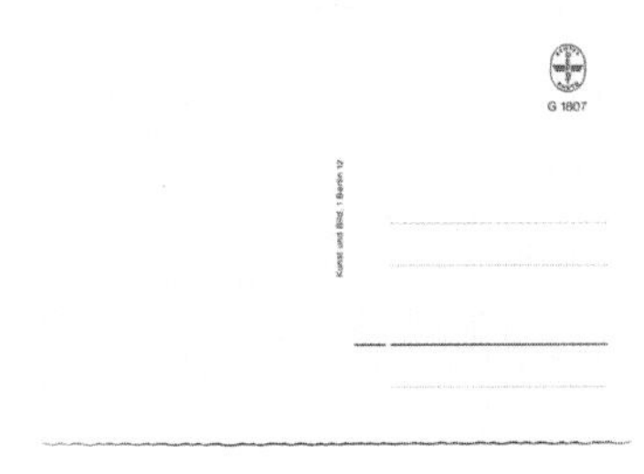

"Checkpoint" at the foreigners' crossing point, Friedrichstrasse

The early barbed-wire fence was replaced quickly by a low wall topped by barbed wire, as shown in this view at Checkpoint Charlie. Note the overhead wires serving the disused tram tracks below.

Berlin, Friedrichstraße

Ausländerübergang Friedrichstr., „Checkpoint“

Berlin, Brandenburger Tor vor dem Mauerbau, 1960

4 039765 060031

Berlin, Brandenburg Gate before the building of the Wall, 1960

The British and Soviet zones met at the Brandenburg Gate in the Pariser Platz, where it was one of the few structures to survive the Second World War intact. This view of a very British looking civilian walking up the Unter den Linden towards the border was taken in the early days of the division of the city – the traffic appears able to go right up to and through the Gate, something that was not possible after August 1961.

Achtung!
Sie verlassen
nach 70m.
West-Berlin
YOU ARE NOW
LEAVING
BRITISH SECTOR

Berlin, Bernauer Strasse

The French zone of West Berlin met East Berlin at Bernauerstrasse. This view shows the first wall under construction in early 1962. At this stage the wall passed close to many, and even incorporated some, apartment blocks and other buildings, as seen on the right of this picture.

FIN
DU
SECTEUR FRANCAIS
Berlin, Bernauer Straße

Untitled

Initially, where the Wall incorporated existing buildings, the lower windows and doors were all boarded up. However, after escapees began to jump from the upper floor windows into West Berlin, all of the windows in the buildings on the east side of the street were bricked up, as shown here in this house in Bernauerstrasse. Later all these houses were demolished, when the area of 'no man's land' was greatly increased.

Berlin, Bernauer Str.

Berlin, Bernauer Strasse, West-Berliner waves over the Wall to East Berlin, 1961

West Berliners could always come up directly to the border, but people were kept far away from the Wall's eastern side. By using ladders they could see over the Wall into East Berlin, where they could wave to their friends or family.

Bernauer Straße
PUHLS

Sebastianstrasse at the corner of Stallschreiberstrasse

In June 1962 the Wall was further extended when a second, parallel fence was created, about one hundred yards behind the first wall, to make escape more difficult by creating a wider area of 'no man's land', sometimes also known as the 'death strip'. Any houses in between were later demolished and the inhabitants relocated.

G 1808

Kunst und Bild, 1 Berlin 12

Berlin, Wilhelmstrasse

Areas behind the Wall were demolished to make way for the building of the second fence further back from the first Wall. From 1965 onwards the stone wall was replaced by one built of concrete. Note the shadows of the photographer and his friends on the western side of the Wall.

WER UNS
ANGREIFT
WIRD
VERNICHTET
Berlin, Wilhelmstraße

Untitled

American President J.F. Kennedy was accompanied by the Mayor of West Berlin, Willy Brandt, and the West German Chancellor, Konrad Adenauer, as they drove to the Rathaus Schöneberg on 22 June 1963. It was on this occasion that Kennedy made his famous speech, in the course of which he said:

> Two thousand years ago the proudest boast was 'civis romanus sum'. Today in the world of freedom the proudest boast is 'Ich bin ein Berliner'. All free men, wherever they may live, are citizens of Berlin, and, therefore, as a free man, I take pride in the words 'Ich bin ein Berliner'.

Later, Kennedy was sometimes accused of having spoken ungrammatically and of having said that he was a doughnut, rather than a citizen of Berlin, but in fact the phrase is grammatically correct, and Kennedy had practised saying it with Willy Brandt before he made the speech. It became one of the most famous phrases of the Cold War.

PRESS

Herausgeber: Arbeitsgemeinschaft 13. August e.V.
im Ausstellungs-HAUS AM CHECKPOINT CHARLIE,
1000 Berlin 61, Friedrichstraße 44, Telefon 251 10 31
Foto: Copyright, auch für nicht kommerzielle Zwecke

„Tunnel 57" (Oktober 1964).
Kind einer flüchtenden Familie
auf dem Schoß eines Fluchthelfers.

Tunnel 57, October 1964

During the Wall's existence, there were around 5,000 successful escapes to the West. One of the methods used was tunnelling, and 'Tunnel 57' was so called because fifty-seven people escaped through it from East to West Berlin in October 1964. It was 140 metres long and was dug from an empty bakery in West Berlin to an unused apartment block in the East. Today, a plaque on the corner of Strelitzerstrasse and Bernauerstrasse commemorates it.

BERLIN
Mahnmal Peter Fechter

2288 C

Kunst und Bild, 1 Berlin 12

Memorial to Peter Fechter

Peter Fechter, aged only 18, was shot by East German guards and bled to death in no man's land in full view of the Western media, when attempting to escape on 17 August 1962. His tragic death aroused outrage and compassion in the Western world, but people who were shot in no man's land could not be helped by Westerners for fear of triggering further fire from the East German guards and thus possibly starting a new world war.

The last person to be killed attempting to cross the Wall was Chris Gueffroy on 6 February 1989.

DIE MAUER, Bernauer Straße

C 3342

Kunst und Bild, 1 Berlin 61, Tel 030 / 251 70 15

The Wall. Bernauer Strasse

Memorials to some of the people who died attempting to cross the Wall. The number of deaths during the period of the Wall's existence is disputed. Some authorities say that as many as two hundred died, but about 160 are certain.

Dorit Schmiel
Ottfried Reck
Ida Siekmann
Bernd Lünser
Rudolf Urban
Ernst Mund
Olga Segler

Berlin, the Wall at Sebastianstrasse, 1963

Despite the grimness of their surroundings, the citizens of Berlin had to carry on with their lives as best they could. An entire generation of children grew up, playing in the shadow of the Wall.

Berlin, Protest am früheren innerstädtischen Grenzübergang Chausseestraße, 1962

Protest at the former inner city border crossing at Chaussestrasse, 1962

Throughout the period of the Wall's existence Berliners on both sides were separated from their families and friends. The placard held by this young West Berliner, protesting at the Wall, reads: 'We West Berliners have the right to visit our friends and loved ones in East Berlin'.

WIR WESTBERLINER
HABEN DAS RECHT,
UNSERE FREUNDE
UND LIEBEN IN
OST-BERLIN ZU
BESUCHEN

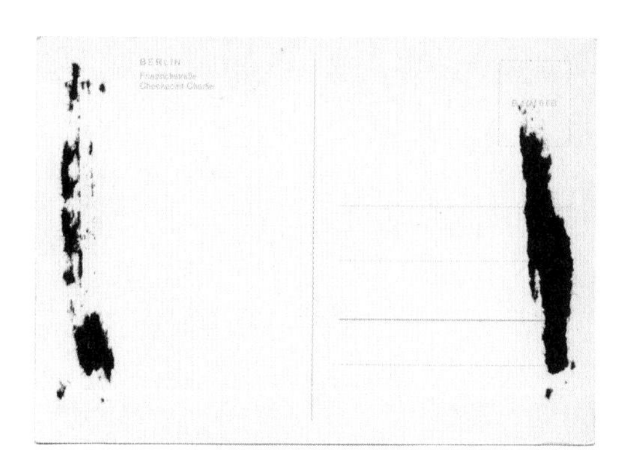

Checkpoint Charlie

By the late 1960s or early 1970s, more of the land between West and East Berlin had been cleared and the border control point at Checkpoint Charlie was enlarged.

ALLIED
MILITARY POLICE
TAXI
YOU ARE LEAVING
VOUS SORTEZ
10km

G 1925

Kunst und Bild, 1 Berlin 12

Berlin, Bernauer Strasse

A view of Bernauerstrasse, where the buildings on the south side of the street were incorporated into the Wall, with their windows bricked up to prevent people jumping from them into West Berlin. Later, as the Wall grew in size and sophistication, these buildings would all be demolished.

Berlin, Bernauer Straße

Berlin, Potsdamer Platz

Before the War, Potsdamer Platz had been the busiest traffic intersection in the whole of Europe and the centre of the city's nightlife. It was surrounded by cafés, clubs, department stores, and the world's largest restaurant, which claimed to seat 8,000 people. During the War it was devastated, first by British and American air raids, and then by artillery fire during the final Soviet assault on Berlin in 1945. The line dividing East from West Berlin ran right through the centre of the square. At first marked by a line of white paint on the street, by the time of this picture the Wall had been built across the square. The buildings that had survived the War became derelict and were gradually demolished as the area of no man's land was enlarged, and the square became filled with rubble and weeds.

Potsdamer Platz
Berlin, Potsdamer Platz

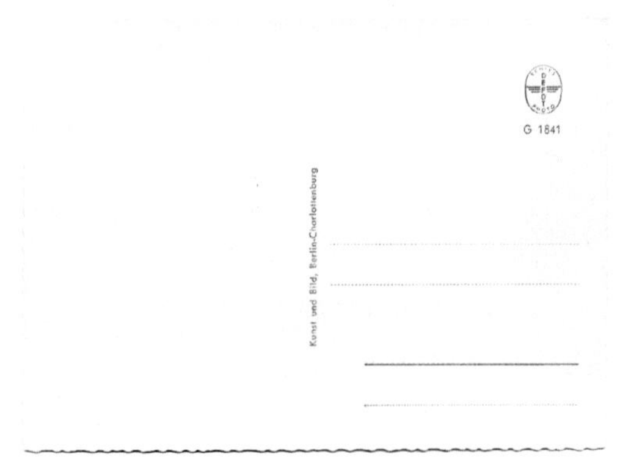

Berlin, Sebastianstrasse

East German guards patrolled the border regularly in motorized convoys. This early view is from the Kreuzberg district of Berlin.

Berlin, Sebastianstraße

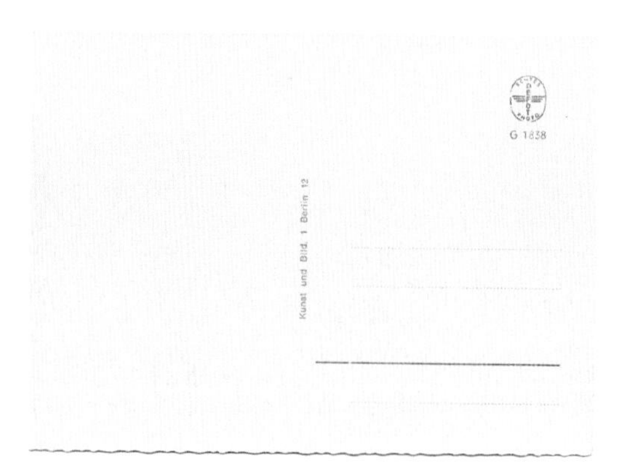

Berlin, Potsdamer Platz

This view of Potsdamer Platz shows the first wall with the anti-tank traps and second fence behind. Note the disused tram tracks in the foreground, and the subways leading to the closed S-bahn station. The division of Berlin had a major impact on the city's public transport network. During the period of the Wall's existence, some sections of the U-bahn were closed or the lines truncated. The S-bahn remained open but where lines crossed from West to East Berlin and back again the stations were closed and the trains ran through without stopping. These stations became known as 'Ghost stations' (Geisterbahnhöfe), and when they were reopened after 1989, it was found that they had become time capsules, even the advertising posters on the walls surviving untouched since 1961. Potsdamer Platz, on the main north–south line of the S-bahn, was the last of these stations to reopen, on 3 March 1992.

Berlin, Potsdamer Platz

Berlin, Ausbau der Grenzanlagen/Mauer
am Potsdamer Platz, April 1976
[illegible]

4 039765 060789

Berlin, Expansion of the border wall at Potsdamer Platz, April 1976

From 1975 onwards the East German authorities constructed the final version of the Wall. Known as Grenzmauer 75 (Border Wall 75) it was made of large free-standing, L-shaped concrete slabs. This card shows it under construction, and the wide area of no man's land behind it is also clearly visible.

PHOTONET.DE

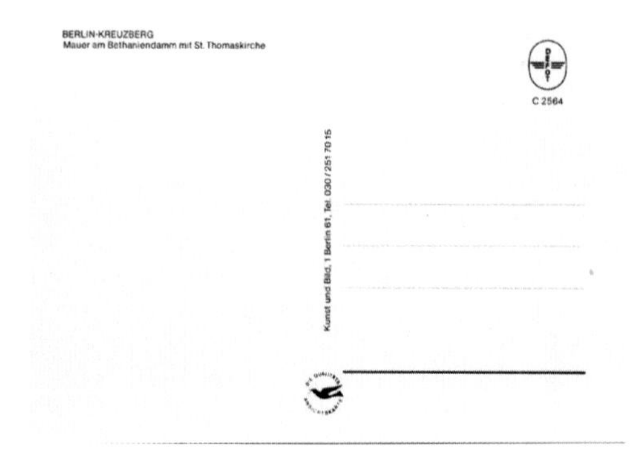

The Wall at Bethaniendamm with St Thomas's Church

A view of the second version of the Wall in the Kreuzberg district of Berlin. Note the smooth, rounded coping stones, which were intended to make it harder for anyone trying to climb over the Wall.

Berlin, the Wall at the corner of Bernauer Strasse and Schwedter Strasse, 1965

Behind the Wall a large hoarding was erected to prevent East Berliners seeing into the West, even with the aid of stepladders, as shown in an earlier postcard. The construction of the first wall, or 'Anti-Fascist Protective Rampart', as it was called by the Soviet newspaper *Pravda*, made contact between citizens living on either side of the border even more difficult.

PHOTONET.DE
Bernauer Straße

Berlin, DDR-Grenzsoldaten an der Mauer am Potsdamer Platz, 1965

4 039765 160212

East German border guards on the Wall at Potsdamer Platz, 1965

East German border guards keeping watch with rifles, binoculars and cameras. The round 'pipe' at the top of the Wall is again prominent in this view.

+++ Berlin +++ Mauer +++ DDR-Soldaten +++ 1965 +++

BERLIN
Sektorengrenze Wilhelmsruh

C 2410

Kunst und Bild, 1 Berlin 12

The Wilhelmsruh Border Sector

This chilling night-time view shows two of the early watchtowers which were replaced in the 1960s. By 1989 there were 300 watchtowers that were erected at intervals along the Wall.

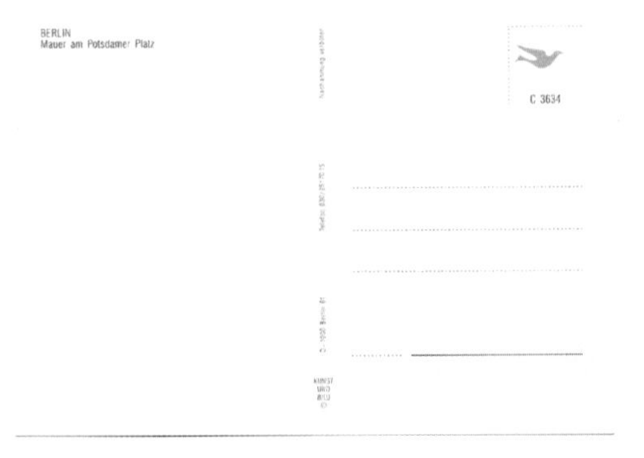

The Wall at Potsdamer Platz

The two faces of the Wall came to reflect the competing ideologies of West and East. The western side became covered with grafitti, an expression of individual liberty that was in stark contrast to the unadorned concrete on the eastern side, which seemed to reflect the grey uniformity of Communism.

GOD LOVES YOU
MIR AUF DIE MAUER AM
1+2. Nov. J RUNNINGS
VISIT

BERLIN
Die Mauer

defot
WERKSTÄTTEN
Nr. C 3689

© Kunst und Bild · 1000 Berlin 61 · Tel. 030 / 251 70 15 – Nachahmung verboten
Photo by Paul Swart

Berlin, The Wall

This is in Pankow, in the north of Berlin – rarely photographed and even more rarely published. It is a view into the deathship, showing the hinterland wall and the electrified signalling fence. The border wall is hidden by the railway dam on the right.

BERLIN
Die Mauer

HAUS AM CHECKPOINT CHARLIE - Ausstellungen:
- "DIE MAUER - vom 13. August bis heute"
- "Maler interpretieren DIE MAUER"
- "BERLIN - von der Frontstadt zur Brücke Europas"
- "VON GANDHI BIS WALESA - Gewaltfreier Kampf für Menschenrechte"

Foto: Cobra / Silberbach Nr. 60

Ronald Reagan am 12. Juni 1987 vor dem Brandenburger Tor: "Herr Gorbatschow, reißen Sie diese Mauer nieder!" - 1990 ist es soweit...

Haus am Checkpoint Charlie, Friedrichstr. 44, 1000 Berlin 61, Tel.: (030) 251 10 31

Ronald Reagan on 12 June 1987 at the Brandenburg Gate: "Mr Gorbachev, tear down this wall! – 1990 has arrived …"

In June 1987, at the Brandenburg Gate, President Ronald Reagan made one of the most famous speeches of the Cold War, when he appealed directly to the Soviet leader Mikhail Gorbachev: 'General Secretary Gorbachev, if you seek peace, if you seek prosperity for the Soviet Union and Eastern Europe, if you seek liberalization, come here to this gate. Mr Gorbachev, open this gate.
Mr Gorbachev, tear down this wall!'.

The significance of the speech remains disputed. At the time the Soviet news agency TASS called it 'an openly provocative war mongering speech', but two years later Gorbachev's impatience with the East German government and his unwillingness to use military force to defend the satellite governments of Eastern Europe were key factors in causing the Wall to be opened.

This card depicts Mr and Mrs Reagan viewing an opening in the Wall during their return visit to Berlin in September 1990. On this occasion Reagan was presented with a large piece of the Wall, which can now be seen at the Reagan Presidential Library in California.

Berlin. Die Mauer / The Wall / Le Mur.

Idee: Edition Lawine, Berlin-Kreuzberg
Foto: Alfred Folkers

„Allez hopp"

"Allez Hopp"

Grafitti depicting Humpty Dumpty on the Wall, probably dating from the 1980s, when the Soviet Union and the United States were engaged in arms limitation talks. The message is that true détente cannot take place as long as the Wall exists.

Détente
all the King's horses, and all the King's men
couldn't put Humpty together again.

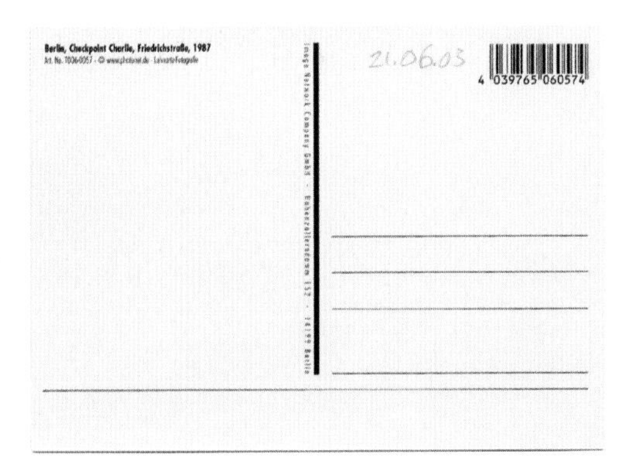

Berlin, Checkpoint Charlie, Friedrichstrasse, 1987

By the 1980s, the original wooden hut at Checkpoint Charlie had been replaced by a more substantial structure. At this time there was no hint that the Wall, and the division of Berlin, would last no more than another two years.

PHOTONET.DE
ALLIED
CHECKPOINT CHARLIE
YOU ARE LEAVING
THE AMERICAN SECTOR
ВЫ ВЫЕЗЖАЕТЕ ИЗ
АМЕРИКАНСКОГО СЕКТОРА
VOUS SORTEZ
SIE VERLASSEN DEN AMERIKANISCHEN SEKTOR

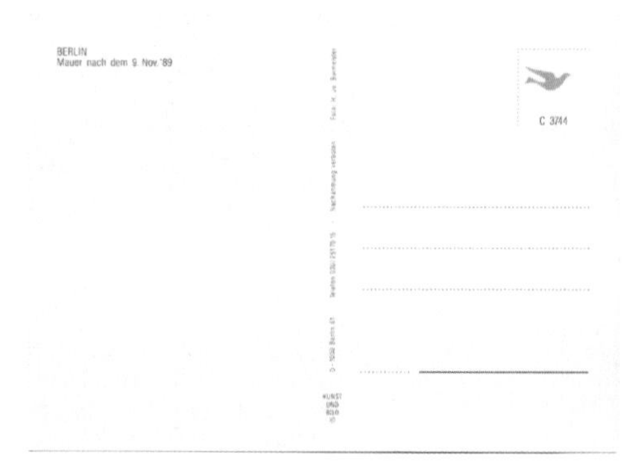

A peek through Berlin: the Wall after 9 Nov. '89

The fall of the Berlin Wall followed the opening of the border between Hungary and Austria in September 1989. As large numbers of East Germans used this as a route to the West, and mass meetings in East Germany itself began to demand a liberalization of the travel laws, the East German government began to consider ways of stabilizing the situation. At a news conference that was broadcast live on the evening of 9 November, a badly-briefed member of the government, Günter Schabowski, announced that foreign travel through any border crossing to West Germany was now possible without advance notice. Unintentionally, the Wall had been opened, and crowds began to gather at the crossing points. At 10.30pm the one located in Bornholmer Strasse became the first to open, soon followed by others. Within hours, fifty thousand East Berliners had crossed over, passing confused border guards who, having received no clear orders, did not intervene.

Something of the sense of both wonder and bewilderment felt by ordinary citizens at this sudden change can be seen in the expression of this soldier, peering through one of the first breaches in the Wall.

Durchblick BERLIN

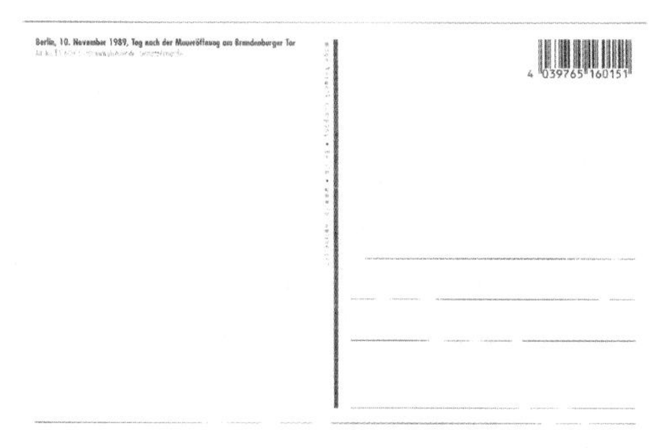

Berlin, 10 November 1989, the day after the opening of the Wall at the Brandenburg Gate

In the first days after the reopening of the Wall, the citizens of Berlin reclaimed their city, by climbing on top of it in a symbolic occupation.

The Brandenburg Gate itself was not reopened until 22 December, when the West German Chancellor, Helmut Kohl walked through to meet his East German counterpart, Hans Modrow, on the other side. Modrow spoke for the many thousands of people present when he said:

> The Brandenburg Gate is not just one of many. The burning stench of war must never be smelt here. It must be a gate of peace.

This statement was particularly significant, as, despite being used as a symbol by the Nazis, the Brandenburg Gate was originally designed as an emblem of peace in the late eighteenth century. The gate is crowned by victory in her chariot, and the gate was part of the Customs wall encircling Berlin.

+++ Berlin +++ Mauerfall +++ Brandenburger Tor +++ 1989 +++

BERLIN
DDR-Grenzpolizisten auf dem Platz vor dem Brandenburger Tor, 10. November 1989 · GDR border police on the square in front of the Brandenburg Gate, 10 November 1989 · Policias de fronteras de la RDA en la plaza delante de la Puerta de Brandeburgo, 10 de noviembre de 1989

Photo: bpk Berlin · © publicon Verlagsgesellschaft mbH · Am Festungsgraben 1 · 10117 Berlin

publicon
B 120

Berlin, the Reichstag, 10.11.89

The Wall by the Reichstag became a focal point for crowds that congregated in the first few weeks of November 1989 to celebrate the fall of the Wall. Although thousands of East Berliners crossed over into West Berlin during this period, few of them intended to stay in the West permanently, the majority returning home at the end of each day. Some never went more than a few yards into the West, seeing the ability to travel freely more as a fundamental human right than as a means of emigrating permanently.

Berlin, 10. November 1989, Tag nach der Maueröffnung am Brandenburger Tor

Art. No. 1006-0016 · © www.photonet.de · Lehnartz-Fotografie

Image Network Company GmbH · Hohenzollerndamm 152 · 14199 Berlin

3.6.00

Berlin, 10 November 1989, the day after the opening of the Wall at the Brandenburg Gate

A close up view of some of the crowds – predominantly of young people – who climbed onto the Wall in the heady days of early November 1989. One US Army intelligence officer wrote:

> The feeling in the air was electric, as if some great force had been let loose, perhaps the greatest example of positive human will ever seen.

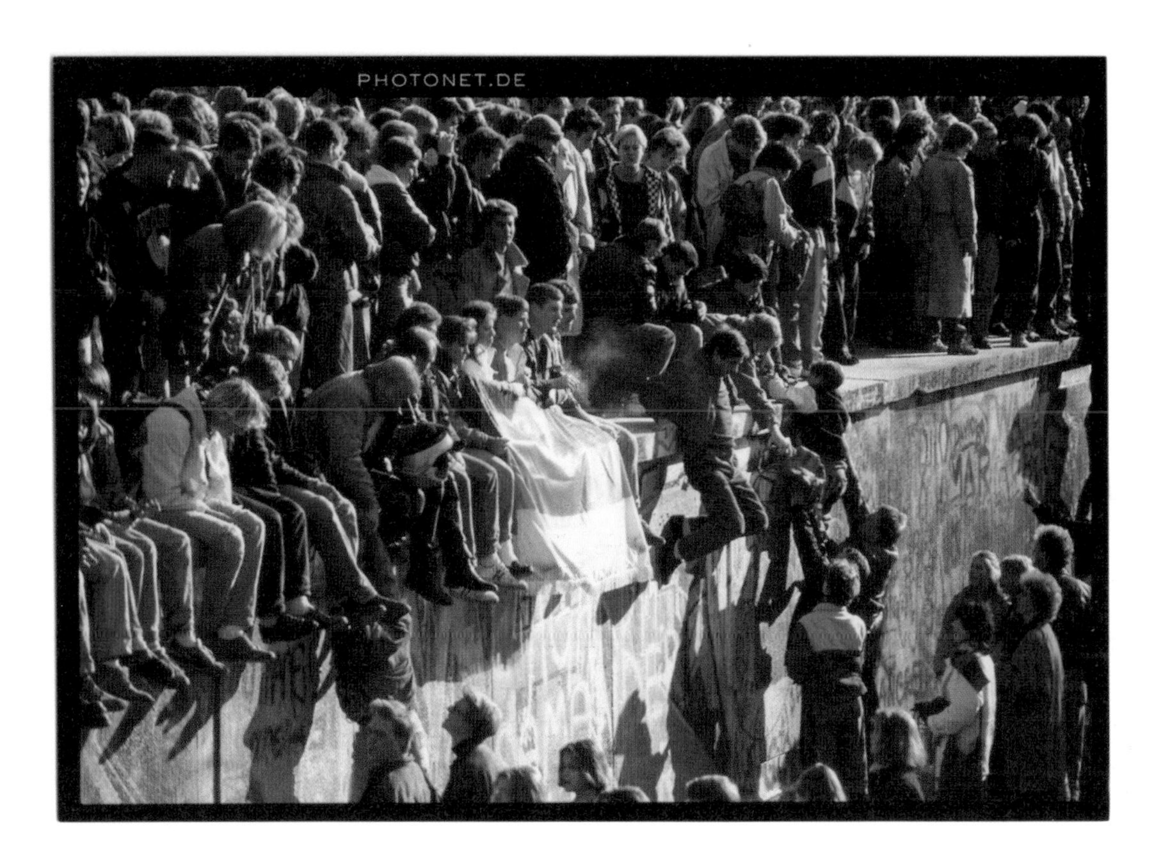
PHOTONET.DE

"Come together"
BERLIN, Brandenburger Tor, 22.12.1989
Photographiert von DIETMAR KATZ

"Come Together", Berlin, Brandenburg Gate, 22.12.1989

The Wall continued to be a focal point in the months ahead, drawing crowds from East and West as the momentum for change gathered pace. The message in this banner conveyed an understanding on the part of its authors of the power of mass movements and foreshadowed German reunification just nine months

COME
TOGETHER

Nr. 140 Berlin nach dem 9.11.1989
© Wolfgang Skowronski

SKOWRONSKI & SZELINSKI VERLAG
Berlin · Telefon (030) 213 69 66

Berlin after 9.11.1989

The car in the foreground is a Trabant. First produced in East Germany in 1957, around three million were made before the production line closed down in 1991, and it became as much a symbol of Communism as the Wall itself. Although not made of cardboard, as was often alleged at the time, its poor performance and smoky two-stroke engine contrasted badly with the Volkswagens, Mercedes, and BMWs being made in the West. For weeks after 9 November, people on the western side of the Wall would stand and cheer each Trabant that crossed over from the East.

In the background can be seen early examples of 'Mauer-Spechte' ('wall peckers'), chipping away at the Wall with hand-held tools. Much of the initial demolition of the Wall was carried out in this unofficial, ad hoc, way.

Tom K.
Stinnes BauMarkt

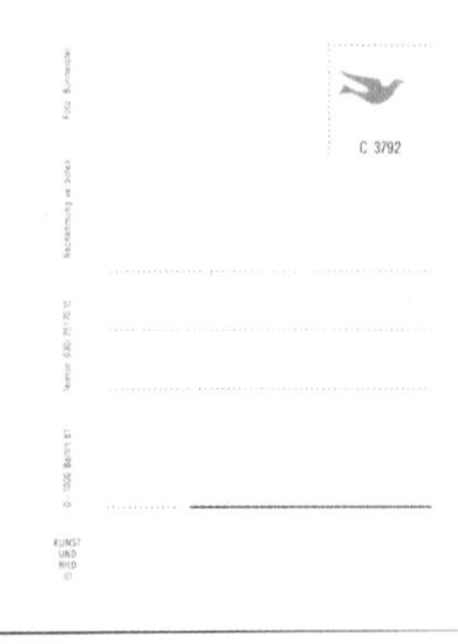

Charlie New Look

The 'wall peckers' became increasingly bold, and in this view the damage done to the Wall through unofficial attempts at demolition can clearly be seen. To the right two people can be seen carrying away a large piece from the top of the Wall as a souvenir.

Pieces of the Berlin Wall can now be found all over the world, as far away as California or Cape Town.

CHARLIE
NEW
LOOK

Berlin nach dem 9.11.1989

Pavel Šima

Berlin after 9.11.1989

An East German border guard casts a slightly wary eye over some 'wall peckers' at work in the shadow of the Reichstag.

In the first few months after the opening of the Wall, some East German border guards attempted to repair some of the damage, and to restrict movement across the Wall to the official crossing points, but this became an increasingly futile exercise as the movement towards full German reunification gathered pace.

Goodbye Charlie!: Checkpoint Charlie—removal on 22.6.1990

Removal of the guardhouse from Checkpoint Charlie was relatively easy as the Americans had never built a permanent structure. The original building was preserved and can now be seen at the Allied Museum at Zehlendorf in the city suburbs.

A replica of an older version was later erected at the former control point, and near to the site is the Haus am Checkpoint Charlie, a museum installed in the late 1960s to protest against the Wall. It has not changed greatly since 1989.

Tschüß
Charlie!
BRANDT

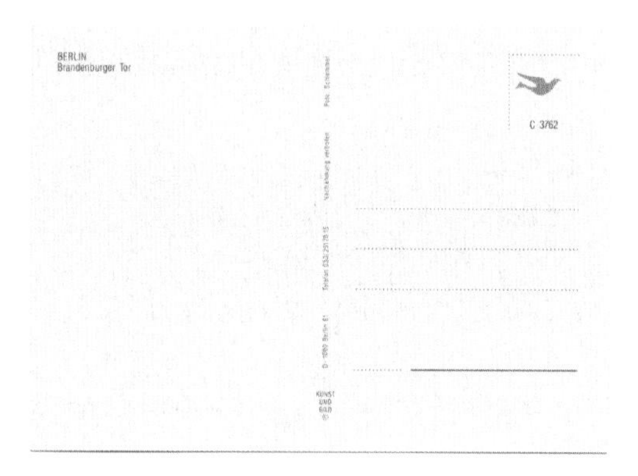

Demolition of the Wall between the Reichstag and the Brandenburg Gate (20.2.1990)

While many unofficial breaches were made in the Wall during the first three months following its opening, official dismantling did not begin until 13 June 1990 in Bernauerstrasse, and was completed only in November 1991. A few short sections were left as a memorial.

The former route of the Wall in the centre of the city is now marked by a line of stones in the street. While the city has been physically reunited, the mental scars remain.

Am Brandenburger Tor – Die Mauer fällt!

3 October 1990: Berlin, the Brandenburg Gate

With the fall of the Berlin Wall, the question of union between East and West Germany rose to the top of the political agenda. As increasing numbers of people travelled to the West in the months after November 1989, the survival of the GDR seemed unlikely. On 23 August, the GDR parliament voted to dissolve the GDR, which paved the way for German reunification on 3 October 1990.

A month earlier, the four occupying powers, together with the GDR and the FRD, signed the so-called 'Two Plus Four Treaty' in which the US, USSR, Britain, and France, renounced their rights under the Instrument of Surrender signed at the end of the Second World War, thus officially restoring full sovereignty to Germany. The division of Germany, conceived in Potsdam in 1945, had finally ended.

3. Oktober 1990

Photo credits. Cover image: Heinz Krimmer © Voller Ernst; pp. 10, 14, 94: © Bildarchiv Preußischer Kulturbesitz; pp. 28, 34, 38, 40, 46, 52, 54, 62, 64, 66, 68, 72, 78, 80, 82 (photo: Paul Swart), 90 & 102 (photo: H. Jo. Burmeister), 106 (photo: Okon): Kunst und Bild; pp. 20, 22, 50: Museum Haus am Checkpoint Charlie; p. 24: © akg-images; p. 26: © akg-images / ullstein bild; p. 84: © Frank Silberbach / akg-images; pp. 30, 32, 36, 42, 56, 58, 70, 74, 76, 88, 92, 96: © photonet.de; p. 86: © Alfred Folkers; p.98: photo: Dietmar Katz; p. 100: © Wolfgang Skowronski; p.104: photo: Pavel Sima; pp.108, 110: © Herbert Schlemmer.